W9-AHP-513

changed

making sense of your own or a loved one's abortion experience

Michaelene Fredenburg

Copyright © 2008 Perspectives

Any opinions, conclusions or recommendations expressed in the material are those of the author and do not necessarily reflect the views of Perspectives.

All rights reserved. No portion of this book may be reproduced, stored in a retrieval system, or transmitted in any form or by any means—for example: electronic, mechanical, photocopy, recording, scanning, or other—except for brief quotations in critical reviews or articles, without the prior written permission of the publisher.

Published by Perspectives
P.O. Box 600533
San Diego, CA 92160

Fredenburg, Michaelene
Changed: making sense of your own or a loved one's abortion experience / Michaelene Fredenburg.
ISBN 978-0-9800633-0-1

Jacket design: Lisa Toscani
Lis@ToscaniDesigns.com

Book design: Candyce Lee Smith
pinkapplefont@gmail.com
www.pinkapplefont.com

Persons depicted are models.

Printed in the United States of America and China

Dedication

My Mom
Penny Lynn Peterson
1946–2006

Table of Contents

Appreciation

Thanks to all who shared their stories in the hope
that it will help someone else.

Thanks also to—

Betsy...for your selfless dedication

Candyce...for designing this book

Dad...for listening, discussing, believing, and of course—for being my dad!

Diaga...for your compassion

Dietrich...for being you

Digitaria...for making our dream of a safe online community a reality

Dr. Strauss and Dr. Venter...for your professional consultation

KarenJoy and Melissa...for your candor and amazing thoughts

Kris...for your enthusiasm

Laura...for your guidance and expertise

Linda...for everything

Lisa...for your amazing talents

Margot...for your confidence in the outreach and in me

Michael...for your love and patience

Suzanna...for your hard work, support, and vision

Teresa...for your resource research

Zack...for inspiring me

Welcome

Welcome

Over the years I've heard many heartrending stories about abortion.

Although each story is unique,
a common thread moves through them all—

abortion changes you.

Yet it is difficult to find a safe place
to help abortion participants
—and those who are closest to them—
explore this tragic truth.

> *I am troubled by the increasing polarization of the abortion debate—a debate that tends to hinder reasoned discussion and keep those who are personally touched by abortion from reaching out.*

I primarily wrote this book for those who are touched by abortion.

However, I hope that people who haven't been personally touched by abortion will read this book as well.

The purpose of this book is threefold:

- Communicate to those who've been touched by abortion that they are not alone
- Heighten awareness of an abortion's impact on various family members and friends
- Create a place of safety for participants to begin exploring their feelings and seeking resolution

YOU ARE NOT ALONE

At current abortion rates, one in three women in the United States will have had an abortion by age 45.[1]

That means a significant percentage of men will have also participated in abortion—
either knowingly or unknowingly.

Although abortion has touched many of us,
we rarely share our personal experiences.

[1] S. K. Henshaw, "Unintended Pregnancy in the United States," Family Planning Perspectives, 1998, 30(1): 24–29, 46; and AGI, "State Facts About Abortion: Texas," http://www.guttmacher.org/pubs/sfaa/texas.html (accessed Feb. 16, 2006).

Shame or guilt may play a role in hiding our abortions.
And the rancorous public debate certainly doesn't encourage dialogue
about this personal and extremely sensitive topic.
We sometimes lack the language to discuss the conflicted emotions
that trouble us.

Whatever the reason,
silence perpetuates the myth that we stand alone in our abortion experiences—
or at least that we're alone amidst the emotional debris.

HEIGHTEN AWARENESS OF AN ABORTION'S IMPACT

In addition to the tens of millions of men and women
who've experienced abortion firsthand,

there are countless other family members,
such as the woman's parents and her children,
who are also impacted by the decision to abort.

It is rare for someone not to know a family member or friend
who's had an abortion.

Regardless of whether or not a person's family members or friends
were directly involved in the abortion decision,
they are still touched by it.

Grandparents,
aunts,
uncles,
cousins,
and siblings
are left grappling with the loss of a family member—
a loss that typically isn't openly acknowledged.

They may also be disturbed by the emotional fallout they observe
in the woman
or in her partner.

They often feel helpless and confused.

How do you grieve a loss that isn't acknowledged by our culture?

How do you reach out to someone you love without causing them more pain?

CREATE A PLACE OF SAFETY

Many men and women are seeking to make sense of their own or a loved one's abortion experience.

I hope this book will aid them in their search by creating—

- A place of safety in which to consider the impact of abortion
- A place where they can explore their feelings and identify their losses
- A place removed from politics and activism and labels

This book seeks to convey the real experiences of real people.

I invite you to begin by reading and reflecting upon the following voices.

And as you read, I hope you'll be able to address your own emotions regarding abortion
and to gain a better understanding of what others have experienced.

I also hope the stories in this book will begin to equip you with new language

so you're better able to
sensitively and compassionately
communicate with others about abortion.

Although the stories in this book are real, I've chosen to conceal the true identities of the people involved. Because abortion touches multiple family members and friends, it's unlikely that all those who've been impacted will reach a place of healing and wholeness simultaneously. Just as their loss and pain are tragic and real, their timelines for healing are also varied and unique. Therefore, the healing process shouldn't be forced or interrupted. Further information about healing can be found in later chapters, starting with the chapter called "Healing Pathways."

—Michaelene

welcome

VOICES

1 "My Child Would Have Been 22 This Year"

“My Child Would Have Been 22 This Year”

MICHAELENE

As a teenager, I assumed legalized abortion was necessary for women to attain their educational and career goals. So it’s not surprising that when I became pregnant at 18, I thought about having an abortion.

The abortion would allow me to continue teaching ballroom dance and training for competition.

The idea of adoption did cross my mind.

I knew I wasn’t ready to parent, but I thought perhaps I could delay my career for the nine months or so that it would take me to carry the baby to term.

My 28-year-old live-in boyfriend was furious when he discovered I was pregnant.

He immediately demanded that I have an abortion.

When I brought up the possibility of adoption,
he yelled at me.
He said he wasn't going to let his colleagues see him with a pregnant girlfriend.

He threatened to kick me out.

I sobbed uncontrollably—I couldn't believe what I was hearing.

In an instant, I realized how stupid I'd been.

Even though I'd met him just a few months earlier while he was visiting our mutual friend, I believed him when he said he loved me. I was so flattered when he urged me to move in with him. Without any more thought, I sought a job at a dance studio near his house, packed my belongings, and moved to another state.

I couldn't go back to my parents now!

I knew they would support me if I carried the baby to term, but I was desperate to make it on my own. The thought of returning home was utterly humiliating. On the other hand, my naiveté concerning this guy was equally humiliating.

I didn't have any other friends or contacts in the area, so I decided to seek advice from the studio manager.

After I told her about my situation, she recommended abortion.

She said it was the only logical option and offered to arrange one for me. I numbly nodded my head, and she made some calls. I left her office with the date and time of the appointment and an arranged ride from my supervisor.

My experience at the abortion clinic was painful and humiliating—nothing like I'd imagined.

Although the young women awaiting their abortions were anxious and tearful, the clinic staff was cold and aloof.

As I lay alone in the procedure room, I could hear footsteps move down the hall and turn in to a room.

This was repeated several times,
each time the footsteps were louder and closer.

My anxiety steadily built and then peaked when the abortion provider and her assistant entered my room.

It was not an empowering experience.

I was completely unprepared for the emotional fallout after the abortion. I thought the abortion would erase the pregnancy. I thought I could move on with my life.

I was wrong.

Although I didn't feel this way before the procedure, it was now clear to me that the abortion ended the life of my child. I felt guilty and desired punishment.

I deserved to suffer.

The mere presence of my boyfriend caused deep hurt and pain.

I found it difficult to work.

In between student lessons, I'd retreat to the staff room and cry.

I soon found myself in a cycle of self-destructive behavior that included an eating disorder.

Desperate for a fresh start, I broke up with my boyfriend, quit my job, and moved from the Midwest to Hawaii.

Although Hawaii was breathtakingly beautiful and bursting with life, I felt dead inside. It didn't take long for me to realize I couldn't escape from myself.

About two years after the abortion, I was living in Southern California when I began experiencing periods of intense anger followed by periods of profound sadness.

For weeks and sometimes months at a time, I was too fatigued to do more than eat a meal and shower during the day.

I lost interest in food, and my weight fell dangerously low.

There were also periods when I seemed able to pull myself together and lead a normal life—at least outwardly.

I saw a number of doctors for the fatigue and weight loss. They tested me for everything from lupus to cancer to AIDS.

I didn't tell them about the feelings
I was having as a result of the abortion.
I didn't see a connection between
the abortion and my current physical symptoms.

This downward spiral continued until suicidal thoughts began to scare me. That's when I finally went to see a therapist.

With the help of counselors and supportive friends, my time of self-condemnation and self-punishment
came to an end.

I was finally able to enter into a healthy grieving process.

As I grieved the loss of my child, I slowly became aware of how my choice to abort had impacted my family…a choice they only learned about when I decided to go public with my experience.

I was surprised and saddened that my parents, my sister, and even my children struggled to deal with the loss of a family member through abortion.

In addition to coping with the fallout that the abortion has caused in my family, there are still times that are painful for me.

After all, healing doesn't mean forgetting.

Mother's Day is particularly difficult.

The year my child would have graduated from high school was also filled with pain.

My best friend's daughter graduated that year. Each time she talked about senior class activities, I was reminded that my child would not be participating.

If my child had gone to college, she would have graduated this year.
This child would now be a young woman with gifts and abilities,
hopes and dreams…

her whole life ahead of her.
There will always be a hole in my heart—
a hole in the fabric of our family and our community.

My child would have been 22 this year.

— Michaelene

“I Thought I Was Helping My Girlfriend” 2

"I Thought I Was Helping My Girlfriend"

ZACK

I nervously waited in the little room.
Did I really want to do this?
Was it going to hurt?
How long would it take?

I was eager to join my friend Linda so we could have lunch at the Thai restaurant down the street. She looked very out of place when I left her in the lobby surrounded by pictures of tattoos.

My head swung around as a man in his mid-twenties confidently strode into the room. With his interesting ear piercings and tattoos that covered his arms and disappeared under his shirtsleeves, he fit right into the décor of the body-piercing salon.

His kind brown eyes immediately picked up on my nervousness.

He introduced himself as Zack, and he asked me where I wanted the piercing. Zack approached the examining table where I was sitting. As he marked the spot on my tragus (the small piece of thick cartilage that projects immediately in front of the ear canal), he assured me that I'd only feel a little pressure.

Then he pulled on a pair of latex gloves and tried to put me at ease with a little small talk.

We chatted easily until the topic of abortion came up after he asked me about my job. Zack's reaction surprised me.

"I don't think abortion should be illegal,
but people need to know that abortion forever changes you."

Zack continued, "I just wrote a paper for school, and I argued that there need to be organizations that offer people full information about abortion. I said these organizations should get government funding."

He paused.
Then he pulled off the latex gloves,
took a deep breath,

and looked me straight in the eyes.

He said,
"I was involved in an abortion."

As Zack paced back and forth in the little room, his story came out. His voice was laden with emotion. He would occasionally pause and pull on another set of latex gloves, only to tug them off again and throw them away before continuing his story:

"When my girlfriend told me she was pregnant, I knew the baby was mine; I knew I'd take care of it. **I loved her.** I wanted to marry her. I would have raised the child alone, if that's what she wanted.

But it was her choice.

I told her I'd help her with whatever she decided.

She said she was having an abortion and that was it.

I didn't feel good about it, but I was determined to support her decision.

When I took her to the abortion clinic, I was the only guy in the waiting room. Five other women were also waiting there, but they were all alone.

I felt weird—out of place. I was also starting to feel angry as I wondered where the other guys were.

I wanted our relationship to last.

I thought having the abortion like she wanted would help.

But we were both changed afterward."

Zack's shoulders slumped, and his gaze fell to the floor.

"I tried to keep us together. I tried so hard. But things kept getting worse until we finally broke it off after two years."

I broke the silence by commenting that many relationships break up after an abortion.

He looked up.

"That makes sense to me…
I wanted it to work, but it didn't."

Then his eyes became troubled.
He leaned toward me and quietly asked,

"Did I do the right thing?"

After a lengthy pause—while the question hung in the air between us—Zack expressed frustration over the lack of information they'd received at the family planning clinic.

"Abortion forever changes you.

It changed my girlfriend,
it changed me
and I've seen it change other women I know."

Gloves pulled on, gloves tugged off. Eyes downcast.
Stillness.

Head up. Tortured eyes looking deeply into mine.

"I carry tremendous guilt about this."

"Zack, there is healing and forgiveness for you."

Doubtful eyes told me I needed to share my story with him. And afterward, once he knew I really did understand,

Zack's relief was evident.
However, he still appeared doubtful about finding peace.

"I don't know if I can forgive myself."

As I began to reassure him, Zack cut me off.

"You don't KNOW how many bad things I've done. I've been on drugs...
My girlfriend and I were occasional users before the abortion, but afterward...
Things got so out of control.

I moved here from Seattle to get away from the stuff I was involved with back there.

My ex-girlfriend is still messed up.
She's usually wasted.
I've tried to help her and talk to her about how the abortion is affecting her,
but it only makes things worse.

I think I'm the worst person to talk to her about it."

After we talked a little more about healing,

I thanked Zack for sharing such a personal story with me.

"No, thank you.
I enjoyed talking with you.
It's hard to talk about abortion.

I can't talk to people who are liberal because abortion is supposed to be okay.
And the people on the Right are scary.

But I can talk to you."

Zack was finally ready to do the piercing.
And he was right—it didn't hurt at all.

— Michaelene

3

"I Never Had the Chance to Know My Brother or Sister"

“I Never Had the Chance to Know My Brother or Sister”

AMBER

The day after I graduated from eighth grade,
my mother had an abortion.

She raised me to be pro-choice, so I really didn’t think much about it.

Well, not until last year.

While my mother was driving me back to college, out of the blue she told me she’d had another abortion while I was growing up.

At first I was shocked,
then I was appalled,
and finally I was angry with her.

I began researching abortion on the Web; and the more I read, the more I came to believe that abortion is bad for women.

Abortion is violent.
Abortion hurts women.
Abortion hurts other family members.

I've spent a lot of time thinking about what it would have been like to have two siblings.

I'm angry with my mother that she would abort them—that she would take them away from me.

I feel like my life as an only child is a lie.

But I also began to understand why my mother struggles with depression. While I was growing up, there were so many times that her bedroom door would be closed, and I could hear her crying in her room.

I feel compassion for my mother;
but at the same time, I am angry with her.

We used to be very close,
but now there is distance between us.

I want to repair the damage to our relationship; but first, I'd need to share how I feel about her abortions.

I'm afraid to do that—

I'm afraid I'll hurt her,

I'm afraid I'll be too angry to control myself.

— Amber

PRISCILLA

My parents are immigrants, and they were very poor when my mom became pregnant with their second baby.

They decided to abort.

They immediately regretted it. And then a couple of years later, they had me.

I've always known about the abortion because my parents often talk about my "other brother" and how guilty they feel about the abortion. I don't know why they believe he was a boy. I don't want to ask them.

My oldest brother doesn't seem bothered by the abortion, but I am.

I think I was the “make-up” baby.

The only reason they had me is because of their guilt over aborting my brother.

I wouldn’t even be alive if they’d kept my brother.

I miss my brother, and I want to give his life meaning.

I try to live my brother’s life for him.

I do this partly for my parents’ sake,
but mostly for the sake of my brother.

Living for him also gives my life value.

I don’t feel that my life has any real worth. I know in my head this isn’t true; but in my heart, I don’t believe I have value. I’m just not convinced—I’m not able to live it out.

I think about my dead brother all the time.

It’s starting to scare me because it doesn’t seem normal. I recently tried to talk to some of my friends about it, but they freaked out. I learned from their reactions to just keep quiet about what's going on inside of me.

I'm able to talk to my boyfriend about it. He listens to me and wants to help, but he doesn't know how. Sometimes I'm scared he'll break up with me over this.

I feel like there is something seriously wrong with me.

Am I crazy?

Is there help for me? Is there healing?

Sometimes I feel hopeful that there is healing,
but mostly I'm afraid to heal.

I'm afraid that if I heal,
I'll forget about my brother.

And if I'm not thinking about him,
then it would be as if he never existed.

— Priscilla

JESSICA, LATANYA, AND MERCEDES

A conversation overheard between three nine-year-old girls…

The girls are waiting in the lobby of the dance studio for their class to start. Each one is dressed in tights and a leotard with her hair neatly pinned in a bun. They alternately sit, kneel, and lie on the floor as they rapidly move from one subject to another.

Latanya: My mom just had an abortion.

Mercedes: What?!

Latanya: My mom just had an abortion.

Jessica: Why did she do that?

Latanya: There are too many children.

Jessica: Why didn't your parents buy a bigger house?

Latanya: There are five kids, so there are seven of us. It's just too many.

Silence

Mercedes: My mom had a baby growing inside her, but it got sick and died.

Latanya: (wistfully) You're lucky then.

4

"My Wife Gets Depressed Around the Anniversary of Our Daughter's Abortion"

“My Wife Gets Depressed Around the Anniversary of Our Daughter’s Abortion”

LISA AND ANN

When my daughter, Lisa, was in college, she became pregnant by an older man.

She called her mother and me for help.

Ann immediately caught a flight to be with Lisa and to help her think through her options. We wanted Lisa to have the baby; but ultimately, she chose to have an abortion.

Ann was devastated by Lisa’s decision.

Maybe if I’d been a better father, this wouldn’t have happened…

My daughter has never gotten over it. Lisa never married, and now it appears that she’ll never have any children. Since Lisa is our only child, that means we’ll never have grandchildren.

I think about the abortion from time to time, and it hurts me to do so. But I must admit—it's much more painful to watch my wife.

Ann has never stopped grieving the loss of our grandchild. Every year on the anniversary of the baby's due date, Ann mourns and struggles with depression.

Yet she won't talk about it with Lisa because she doesn't want to cause our daughter additional pain.

Abortion has profoundly affected our family.
It has changed all of us.

— William

JULIE AND CAROL

When our daughter, Julie, was 16, she began dating a nice boy from her school. She was very happy, and they were so sweet together. Julie was doing well in school, she had lots of friends, and she was generally upbeat about life.

Then sometime during the spring semester, Julie became anxious and distracted.

At first we thought she was just reacting to pressures at school; but as she became more withdrawn, we grew more concerned.

Our attempts to talk with her didn't reveal much.
Julie insisted she was fine.
The more we asked,
the more defensive and secretive she became.

Julie's grades started dropping.
She broke up with her boyfriend,
and she stopped hanging out with her friends.

When she began eating less and sleeping more, we took her to the doctor.
It was clear that she was depressed, but we didn't know why.

Julie was prescribed antidepressants, and she started seeing a therapist. But neither the medication nor the therapy helped. Eventually, Julie stopped taking care of herself and simply lost interest in living.

We were afraid to leave her alone—
we thought she might try to hurt herself.
One night I felt so panicky about Julie's behavior that I

started yelling at her. She began sobbing, and then she told me she'd had an abortion.

I was stunned.

I dropped down next to Julie, and I wrapped my arms around her. I held her tight as the sobs shook her body and left her gasping for breath.

When Julie's sobs diminished,
she tearfully told me how she'd discovered her pregnancy
and how scared she was to tell her father and me.
She said she didn't want to disappoint us
and she didn't want us to know she was having sex.
She told me she'd skipped out of school with her boyfriend to go to the clinic.

My heart hurt for her,
and my tears flowed as freely as hers did.
But I also felt relieved that I finally knew why.
Now that we knew what triggered her depression, I believed she could heal—that our family could heal.

I only wish we'd known sooner—
I wish we could have supported Julie during her time of need.

— Carol

RYAN AND MARY

I was checking the meatloaf in the oven when I noticed my teenage son, Ryan, standing in the doorway of the kitchen. I asked him to set the table before I turned back to finish making the salad.

When I turned back around to set the salad bowl on the table, the table was empty and Ryan was still standing in the doorway.

I was about to scold him when Ryan quietly asked,

"Mom, can Vicki come stay with us?"

"Sure honey, your girlfriend can join us for dinner tonight."

"No Mom, not for dinner—to stay with us,
to live with us for a while."

What on earth…
"Ryan, what are you talking about?"

He dropped his eyes to the floor and remained silent.

"Ryan, what is going on?

He finally lifted his eyes to meet mine.
"Nothing's going on, I just want to know if Vicki can come live with us for a while."

"No, no she can't. She needs to live with her own parents."

"But Mom…"

"No buts. What a ridiculous idea. Vicki needs to be with her parents. Now please set the table, dinner is almost ready."

Shaking my head, I finished the dinner preparations and called the rest of the family in to eat.

Two weeks later, I found Ryan outside my bedroom door.
He looked horrible.
I was immediately alarmed.
"Ryan, what's the matter? Has something happened?"

Ryan tried to talk, but he started to cry.
I reached up to hug him, and he clung to me.
We cried together until Ryan was able to tell me what happened.

"Mom, I got Vicki pregnant. And her parents made her have an abortion."

I gasped.
My heart froze.
And then a terrible thought began to form in my mind…

"Ryan, is this why you asked me if Vicki could live with us?"
All he could do was nod and hang his head.

Oh my God. What had I done? Why hadn't I listened to him? Why didn't I press him to find out the reason behind his seemingly bizarre request?

I felt like a sword had pierced my heart.

I could have saved my grandchild.
I could have saved my son from this grief and pain.

If only I had stopped and paid attention.

If only I had tried to talk to him about it after dinner.

I was listening now.

Ryan told me how he'd tried to help Vicki
when her parents were pressuring her to have the abortion.

He said he was thinking about asking me again if Vicki could live with us, when her parents suddenly—and secretly—took her to the clinic.

He was shocked and devastated,
and now Vicki didn't want to talk to him anymore.

In the months and years that followed, my sorrow only increased as I watched my son suffer.

Ryan's self-confidence evaporated,
he later dropped out of college,
and he meandered from one job to another.
He was so changed.

After many painful years,
Ryan was able to put the abortion behind him.
He's married now. He has three children and a good job.
He's enjoying life.

My pain has decreased over time,
but occasionally something will trigger sharp jabs of guilt and loss.

— Mary

"my wife gets depressed around the anniversary of our daughter's abortion"

"I Thought I Was Helping Her" 5

“I Thought I Was Helping Her”

KAY

I got pregnant at 16.

I immediately decided to have an abortion,
and I asked my friend Jenny if she’d go with me to the clinic.
But Jenny didn’t think abortion was the best option,
and she talked to me about the baby that was growing inside of me.

I didn’t want to hear it at first; but the more I thought about it, the more excited I got.

There was a tiny little baby growing inside of me, and I was its mother.

I was amazed that I was actually starting to consider having the baby.

Jenny and I talked and talked about what it would be like to parent a baby while I was still in high school. Jenny made some good points. She confirmed that it would be difficult. But at the same time, she assured me that I could do it and that she would help me.

By the time I decided to tell my mom about the baby, I was firm in my decision to parent.

Well, not as firm as I thought.

My resolve quickly dissolved in the face of my mother's wrath.

She told me I was only thinking of myself—
that I was being incredibly selfish.

What about the baby?

I was too young to be a mother.

What about my schooling?

I wouldn't be able to get a decent job if I didn't graduate from high school.

What about college?

I'd resent this baby if I had to give up my dreams.

What about my career?

I wouldn't be able to support the baby and myself.

What about our family?

My family's prominence in our small East Coast town would be ruined.

When I protested, she threatened to kick me out of the house.

I was shocked!

But I also love and respect my mom.
In the past she's been correct about what's best for me, so I thought she was probably correct now as well.

It didn't take long for me to switch back to my original decision to abort.

I don't remember much about the clinic or the procedure.

I just remember feeling empty and numb afterward.

I finished high school, but I didn't finish college.
After moving away from home, I became terribly depressed.
I had to undergo therapy for a couple of years before I was able to get my life back on track.

Most of the time I don't think about the abortion.

But each year
Mother's Day is pretty rough.
My baby would have been born around that day.
I always think about how old my child would be.

Now I have hope again—hope for the future.

I'm back in college and
I hope to graduate by the time I'm 30.
I hope to help others by working as a social worker.
I hope I'll get married and have children.

I also hope my mom will someday know that I've forgiven her—

she was just trying to help me.

— Kay

JANET

My parents divorced when I was a child. But even after the divorce, my parents continued to fight. They mostly fought about me, and I was miserable. At 15 years old, I wanted out.

About this time, an older boy started paying attention to me. It made me feel good. Greg asked me out, and I eagerly accepted. We started hanging out and going to movies together.

It was so exciting when he held my hand.
I floated on air for days after our first kiss.

Greg's parents were divorced too. Greg lived with his mom, and she worked a couple of jobs and was rarely home. We started going to his house after school and making out, which soon led to sex. It kind of hurt, but I loved feeling close to Greg—I loved being loved by him.

A couple of months later, I didn't get my period.

I ignored it at first, but when I missed another period and started throwing up, I told Greg about it. We went to a clinic to get a pregnancy test. I kept thinking it would be negative until the nurse came in and told us I was pregnant.

She started talking to us about our options, but I wasn't listening.

I was going to have a baby!

Greg and I could start a new family together.
Maybe I could live at his mom's house until he graduated and got a job.

After we left the clinic, I told Greg what I was thinking. He was a little surprised, but he said he'd take care of me and the baby. He also said I'd need to tell my parents before he talked to his mom.

I didn't think my dad would be happy about the pregnancy, but I wasn't prepared for how angry he was.

There was a lot of yelling and screaming.
He said he wasn't going to let me ruin my life.
He said I was too young to have a baby.

I tried to tell him that Greg would take care of us
and that someday Greg and I would get married.

But Dad wouldn't listen.

He said I was going to have an abortion so I could finish high school.

I told him I wouldn't have the abortion,
but he said I was going to have it anyway—that it was for my own good.

Two days later we were at the clinic.
I cried the entire time.

My dad was calmer by that time, and he tried to make me feel better.

He kept telling me he didn't want me to have to struggle like he did.
He wanted me to get a good education

and a good job,
and he wanted me to marry someone when I was older
so the marriage would last
and so our kids could grow up in one home.

After the abortion I went home and cried myself to sleep. The next day my dad suggested I forget about the abortion, which seemed like a good idea to me. It was all too painful.

I didn't see Greg for a while; but about six months later, we began having sex again. We didn't talk about the abortion, but we were more careful about using protection.

I guess we weren't careful enough because a couple of months later—

I missed my period again.

I waited a few more months before I said anything to anyone. If I really were pregnant, then by the time my dad found out, I hoped it would be too late to have an abortion.

However, when I started throwing up, my dad suspected something was going on, and he took me to the doctor.

He was furious when the doctor confirmed I was pregnant again. This time he told me that if I didn't have another abortion, then he'd have Greg arrested for statutory rape.

What could I do?
I loved Greg.
I didn't want to get him in trouble!

I tried to forget about the second abortion
but I couldn't.

I cried
and I drank
and I started experimenting with drugs.

I hung out by a lake when I was wasted.
I thought about my babies, and I cried.
I stared at the water and thought about how I was dead—

dead like my babies.

I thought about walking into the water and drowning myself,
but something always kept me back from the water's edge.

I didn't finish high school,
and I didn't get a good job.
I'm on my second marriage now,
but I do have three wonderful kids.

I used to blame my dad, but now I understand he was just trying to help me. I want the best for my kids too.

— Janet

"i thought i was helping her"

"I Often Wonder if There Was Something I Could Have Done to Help Her"

6

“I Often Wonder if There Was Something I Could Have Done to Help Her”

BRAD

My wife and I found out she was pregnant shortly after we were married.

Even though we were having some difficulties adjusting to our new life together,

we were both very excited!

We were making plans for the baby,
going to doctors appointments,
and smiling over ultrasound pictures.

We believed the baby was going to be a little boy.
We were going to name him Trevor.

However, just a month later, Tracey began acting very cold and distant.
She began to have troubling dreams.
One morning she told me she'd had a dream in which

Trevor begged her not to do "it."

Do what? Tracey said she didn't know.

I was disturbed by the dream, and I wondered if Tracey was trying to tell me she was thinking about having an abortion. But she'd tell me about it, wouldn't she?

Tracey started suffering from severe morning sickness. When she was very sick, she'd curse the pregnancy.

I was worried about her—
and about the baby.

As the morning sickness continued, Tracey began saying she couldn't go through with the pregnancy. At this point I demanded that she tell me what was going on.

She looked at me defiantly and said, "I'm going to get an abortion. I know how you feel about abortion, but I don't care. I'm having one no matter what you say or do."

Wow! What could I do?
I realized in an instant that I was powerless.

I didn't argue with her; rather, I stayed calm and tried to support her decision.
I secretly hoped that my compassion and prayer would change her mind.

However, when I think about it now,
I think I could have done more to support her
and to help her think through her decision.
I certainly could have reached out to others to seek their advice and resources.

But I didn't do any of that.

Instead, I drove her to the clinic.

The staff at the clinic was upbeat and personable, but I felt terribly depressed. As I looked at all of the young women waiting for their turns, I wondered if they were married or not. All I knew was that I didn't belong there.

When Tracey came out after the abortion, she looked worse than before she went in.

It looked as though the life had been sucked out of her.

I tried to grab her hand to help her to the car.

She glared at me and said, "I don't need your F---ING help."

I took her home, and then I went to the pharmacy to fill her prescription for the bleeding and the pain. I did what I could to make her comfortable.

I often think back and wonder if there was something I could have done to help her. Maybe there was—but I'll never know.

What I do know is that getting an abortion was very easy, but what happened afterward was very hard.

Tracey and I divorced, and we soon lost contact with each other. When I talked to her many years later, she brought up the abortion and started crying. She said she'd gone through therapy.

It took me a long time to come to terms with what happened. When I see little children, sometimes tears spring up in my eyes as I envision Trevor—

my son who never got a chance.

— Brad

MITCH

My girlfriend told me she had an abortion two months after she did it.

She said the baby was mine;
the decision was hers.

I don't even know what to think about that.

I don't know what I would have said
or what I would have encouraged her to do,

but I should have been given the chance!

— Mitch

7

“I Thought Life Would Be the Way It Was Before”

"I Thought Life Would Be the Way It Was Before"

PAM AND VERONICA

During the class discussion after a college lecture, one of the students, Pam, hesitantly stated that some women don't have a negative reaction after an abortion.

In a quivering voice, she went on to describe the circumstances that necessitated her own abortion—
unable to complete college,
a lack of housing,
and abandoned by the baby's father.

Although she was close to tears, she repeatedly stated that she was "okay."

As I fielded more questions, I kept a close eye on Pam.

She appeared to be calming down when another student, Veronica, asked Pam if she'd felt free to choose a different pregnancy option.

Pam's chin began to tremble as the other students started to discuss what Pam should or shouldn't have done.

Before I could intervene and stop this inappropriate and hurtful debate,
Pam started crying and angrily defended herself to Veronica.
Then Veronica became visibly upset, and she also started crying.
Before long, both young women were sobbing,
and most of their classmates were also close to tears.

Thankfully, the professor was able to assist Pam and Veronica after class. Veronica admitted that she'd also had an abortion and was struggling with it. Both students were grateful to have a safe place to talk about the painful emotions regarding both of their abortions.

— Michaelene

JUANITA

My family immigrated to the United States 10 years ago.

Most of them have low-paying jobs.

And I've watched how they struggle to make ends meet.

I want to make a better life for myself.

That's why I stayed in high school when others were dropping out. It's also why I'm attending junior college. After getting my associate's degree, I hope to transfer to a four-year university. Or maybe I'll enter a program to become a physician's assistant.

When I hear some women talk about how
they had a bad experience with abortion,
I feel sorry for them.
But I really can't relate.
I had an abortion last year, and I'm okay.

I wasn't happy to find out that I was pregnant, but I did spend some time gathering information about my options before making a decision.

I think I made the best choice for myself.
It may not be the best choice for others,
but it was for me.

During one of my classes, the topic of abortion came up.

Everyone seemed to have an opinion, including a student who had an abortion and regretted it.

I decided to share my personal story—just to give the other side.

My classmates were cool about it—even the one who regretted her abortion.
She said it was good that I'd received a lot of information; she felt that she didn't get enough beforehand.

One of the guys said he didn't think there'd been enough studies done about the physical and emotional complications. He asked me if I agreed with that.

To be fair, I told him there probably weren't enough studies and perhaps I didn't get all of the medical facts.

Regardless, I emphasized that I still thought I'd made the best decision.

I also told him that the abortion had definitely changed my attitude toward contraception. I shared that I didn't want to have another abortion, so I'm very serious about taking precautions. I encouraged the other students to be careful as well.

This sparked some more discussion about abortion
and pregnancy
and prevention
until the discussion circled back to the negative reactions
that some women have after an abortion.

The student who had the abortion spoke up again, and she said no one told her how difficult Mother's Day would be. She said she's reminded of her missing child, and she mourns the loss of that child.

In spite of myself, I felt the tears spring up in my eyes.

I could feel a lump form in my throat as jumbled emotions began to surface.

I didn't know where they were coming from,
but I suddenly had to admit that I was unprepared to feel anything
other than relief after the abortion.
This was tougher than I expected.

As class ended and the students began to leave the room,
I wasn't able to get out of my seat.
I was surprised to feel actual tears coming down my face.

Why was I feeling this way now?

I saw the professor approach me. She asked me if I wanted to go back to her office to talk. I mutely nodded my head and followed her.

In spite of these new painful emotions,
I was grateful there was someone to help me sort them out.

— Juanita

MINDY

I've never had an abortion,
nor have I ever been pregnant.

But I'm at the age when a lot of my friends are getting pregnant.

Some of them have had miscarriages,
and some of them have had abortions.

So I'm supposed to mourn with my girlfriends who miscarry

and cheer on my girlfriends who choose to abort.

What bothers me the most is that many times
the ones who miscarry
and the ones who abort
are at the same point in their pregnancies.

How can I mourn for one child and be indifferent toward the other?

— Mindy

8

“We Made the Decision Together, but I’ve Never Felt So Alone”

“We Made the Decision Together, but I’ve Never Felt So Alone”

ALEX

I’d graduated from college, I was just starting an exciting career, and I was engaged to a wonderful guy when I found out I was pregnant.

I was shocked at first.
This wasn’t in the plan!

But I was definitely having the baby because I didn’t believe in abortion.

I was a little nervous when I told Ken.
I knew this wasn’t his plan either.
However, I didn’t expect him to coldly suggest I abort the baby.

After all, we were engaged—
we were planning on getting married.
He also knew I was against abortion.

Ken calmly explained that having a baby right now didn't fit into our plans. He said we shouldn't have a baby until we were married, had been working in our careers longer, and were in a better financial situation.

When I protested, he simply repeated the same argument.

His words stung.
I was confused and hurt.
Didn't he love me?

I thought he'd change his mind, so I didn't do anything at first.

But over the next few days, he continued to explain to me why we couldn't have this baby.
In turn I'd gently remind him that we were already planning on getting married and that I really couldn't have an abortion.

His gentle persistence eventually became more forceful.
He tried to convince me that our relationship wouldn't last if I didn't have the abortion.

The more I cried and pleaded, the harder and more

demanding he became.

I didn't want to lose him.
I didn't want our relationship to end.

I began to think maybe he was right. I began to think our relationship couldn't endure the stress of the pregnancy and the birth of a baby.

My arguments grew weaker until I finally gave in to him. I still didn't want to have the abortion—I knew it would end the life of our child. But I thought that if I got it over with quickly—that if I had the abortion early enough in the pregnancy—then I'd be able to cope with it.

I thought I'd be okay—we'd be okay.

I was wrong.
I immediately regretted the abortion.

I felt the loss of our child from the core of my being.
I grieved over my child—our child.

I grieved over my inability to stay true to my beliefs.
I felt off balance.

I felt as though my center was gone.

Ken was frustrated that I cried so often.
His frustration quickly turned to anger.

I would cry,
and he would YELL.

Whenever I tried to tell him how I was feeling, he'd storm out. The distance between us kept growing until we finally broke up two months later.

The loss was unbearable. In fact, the losses were unbearable.

I didn't want to come home to an empty apartment, so I started working more hours.

When I wasn't working, I filled my time with social activities.
As long as I could fill my time with activity—as long as I wasn't alone—

I didn't have to think.

At some point, constantly going to the movies, eating out

with friends, going to clubs, and buying new clothes for my ever-growing social life began to accumulate a hefty price tag. Even though I knew I was spending more than I was making, I kept right on spending.

This was out of character for me.
I'd always been responsible.
I prided myself in how I managed my time, my finances, and myself.

Now that my debt was accumulating and I didn't seem to have the power to stop it, I began to think my entire self-perception was a lie.

I was against abortion,
yet I'd had one.

I thought my fiancé loved me,
but he left me.

I believed in keeping a careful budget,
but now I was in debt.

I used to like who I was,
but now I couldn't stand to be alone with myself.

I hated who I'd become—
or perhaps I was simply getting to know the real me.

The funny thing was no one else knew.

People looked at me and thought I had it all together. I was successful at my job, I had a lot of friends, and I was the life of the party.

No one knew I was spinning out of control.

No one knew I was filled with anger and grief.

No one knew but me.

Right about this time, I went to a business meeting with my boss. I couldn't believe it when the topic of abortion came up.

I felt so many emotions;
but more than anything, I wanted to tell the other women that I was against abortion.

But I didn't dare do it because I'd had one.
Obviously, my abortion exempted me from ever sharing my opinion.

So you can imagine how stunned I was when the woman sitting next to me told the group that she used to favor abortion—until she had one.

She quietly yet confidently said abortion wasn't good for women. My boss agreed with that statement. I was so amazed—I didn't hear the rest of the conversation.

Later that day I did something I never thought possible.

I confided to my boss that I'd had an abortion and that I was having a hard time with it.
Her response was sympathetic and compassionate. She didn't ask me for any details,
but she did suggest that I talk to someone who'd also gone through an abortion.

I thought this was a good idea; and although it was scary and painful, I met with the woman from the business meeting.

It felt good to tell my story to someone who understood.

As we talked, I felt as though I were connecting the dots between

the abortion,
the grief,
the compulsive spending,
and the self-hatred I'd been feeling.

This realization alone was freeing.
I felt hopeful that the cycle I was in would end.
I felt hopeful that healing was possible.

I also found myself telling this woman about my sister's and my mother's abortions. This was a secret I'd carried for a long time. I was surprised by the waves of grief and loss I felt as I talked about my missing sibling and my missing niece or nephew.

I realized with a jolt how much abortion had changed the fabric of my family,
as well as the fabric of my soul.

—Alex

SUSAN AND RANDY

Randy and I were both juniors in college when we got engaged.

I was so happy!
Randy was so smart and so talented and so cute!

We'd been high school sweethearts.
And I'd been dreaming of the day when we'd get married and have a bunch of kids.

Even though we were Christians and we'd made a commitment to wait until marriage to have sex, after the engagement it got harder and harder for us physically. I lost my virginity at the end of summer break.

We felt a little guilty about it, but not too much—
after all, we were getting married.

I began to suspect that I was pregnant a couple of months into our senior year.

I told Randy about it after I took a home pregnancy test.
He was a little shocked, but very sweet.
He said we'd just have to get married a little sooner than

originally planned.

My fears evaporated when I looked into Randy's shining eyes. His love and commitment were obvious.
And we decided to tell our parents over Christmas break.

Their reaction quickly revived my fears.

Both sets of parents immediately urged us to have an abortion. They said that having a baby now would ruin Randy's chance to accept the full-ride scholarship he'd been offered to medical school.

We were unprepared for their persuasive arguments.
But it was clear that they were only trying to help us.

Randy and I both began to doubt our decision to get married early and have the baby.
I certainly didn't want to ruin Randy's dream of being a surgeon.

Hurt and confused, we went to my doctor for the abortion.

We got married that summer, and Randy started medical school in the fall. We waited to have children until after

Randy finished his residency.

We love our children,
and Randy is successful in his field.
But there is always a void in our home
and in our marriage.

I feel horrible when someone comes to our house and
admires its size,
its furnishings,
the pool,
and the tennis courts.

I want to shout at them that the cost was too high!

But instead of saying anything,
I look away with tears in my eyes,
and I think about how our big house
and Randy's successful career
were bought at the expense of our first child.

It's a thought I can't bear to share with Randy.

— Susan

9

“My Mom Is Hurting, and I Don’t Know How to Help Her”

"My Mom Is Hurting, and I Don't Know How to Help Her"

JUSTIN

"Can I talk to you outside?"

I nodded and followed him out of the community college classroom.

We quietly stood on the dimly lit pathway while 18-year-old Justin shuffled his feet uncomfortably.

After clearing his throat several times, Justin looked at me with tears in his eyes and said,

"Something you said pierced me right in the heart.

When you mentioned during the lecture that some women who've had abortions have difficulty bonding with their children,
I suddenly understood why my mother has been so distant from me and my brothers.

I've wanted so badly to be close to my mother.

I've tried so hard.

I thought it was my fault.

But for the first time, I don't think it's my fault."

Justin went on to explain:

"When I was 14, my mother told me she aborted her first pregnancy.

She said she used to be in favor of abortion,

until she had one.

She made it clear that she was telling me this so I would be sexually responsible.

I have been responsible.
But ever since she told me about her abortion,
I've wondered about the brother or sister who is missing.

However, I never thought about how the abortion affected my mother."

Justin began to cry. He tried to quickly wipe away the tears, but they kept coming.

"It all makes sense to me now.

Is there anything I can do to help her?

Is there anywhere she can go for counseling?

Can she get better?

I love her so much."

— Michaelene

HEALING PATHWAYS

Healing Pathways 10

Healing Pathways

Abortion can produce troubling emotions.

You are not alone.

Many
men,
women,
teenagers,
grandparents,
siblings,
other family members,
and friends

are seeking to make sense of their own or their loved one's abortion experience.

This book is a safe place to begin.

You may use this book to

tell your story,
explore your feelings,
identify and grieve your losses,
recognize unhealthy behaviors,
and begin to experience healing.

This book provides a place that is set apart from politics,
from labels,
from debate.
This space and time is yours.

The following chapters are a starting point
for reflection
and healing
regarding the personal impact of abortion.

Although the following chapters suggest a healing pathway,
the process isn't linear.

Healing typically moves in a spiraling cycle—messy circles that tighten and relax over time.

There isn't a set timeline—nor should healing be forced.

Each person will go through the process differently.

I invite you to turn the page and begin your journey.

If you haven't experienced abortion, I encourage you to read through the following chapters so you'll be better able to compassionately assist others who need healing.

Please remember that you cannot force people to heal—they must welcome healing and embark upon the journey themselves. Once the journey has begun, however, they will often need care and support.

Important Note: This book is not meant to take the place of professional counseling. Sometimes an abortion experience can create intense emotions that you may not feel equipped to deal with on your own.

If you have access to the Web, please visit AbortionChangesYou.com and use the Find Help locator to access support resources. If you don't have access to the Web, please use your phone book to locate professional therapists, after abortion healing resources, or church counseling programs in your area. Call the National Suicide Prevention Lifeline at 1-800-273-TALK (8255) if you're thinking about or planning to hurt yourself.

Tell Your Story 11

Tell Your Story

To begin your healing journey, I believe it's necessary to tell your story.

Telling your story will help you start making sense of your own abortion experience or the abortion of someone close to you.

Something very powerful happens when you document events that occur in your life.

It may be difficult or even painful to tell your story.

I remember how difficult it was for me.

Keep in mind that you may need to make several attempts to start or finish it.

That's okay.

Telling your story may stir up powerful emotions, or you

may feel no emotion at all.

There is no right or wrong way to go about it.

The important thing is to tell it—
to acknowledge that your experience is real and that it's significant.

If you've experienced or been touched by more than one abortion, it's helpful to explore the story of each one separately.

This can be particularly painful—as it was for Alex ("We Made the Decision Together") when she told first the story of her own abortion and then later on the stories of her mother's abortion (Alex's brother or sister) and her sister's abortion (Alex's niece or nephew).

Although your story will be unique, remember: You are not alone.

I've included some questions that may help you tell your story. You may wish to use the next few pages or the journal section at the back of this book to write your story, or you may choose to start either an online or a paper journal.

I encourage you to write openly and honestly.
Freely express the truth of your experience.
Don't worry about grammar or neatness.

Since you won't be sharing this journal publicly, you don't need to edit or omit any events, thoughts, or emotions that may be hurtful to the other people who were involved in the abortion(s).

Once you've written your story or stories, please save the journal and keep it in a private place.

Because telling your story is essential to moving forward, you may want to refer back to it while you're working through other healing pathways, such as exploring your emotions or identifying your losses.

This space and time is yours.

QUESTIONS TO CONSIDER IF—

You Experienced Abortion

Before

When did you find out you were pregnant?

Whom did you tell?

What was their reaction?

What options did you consider?

What events led up to your decision to abort?

During

When and where did the abortion take place?

Who accompanied you to the clinic or doctor's office?

What happened there?

After

What happened right after the abortion?

Did you talk to anyone about it?

What happened in the days and weeks that followed?

What happened in the months and years that followed?

What did you feel immediately afterward?

What do you feel now?

How has the abortion impacted your life?

changed

tell your story

QUESTIONS TO CONSIDER IF—

Someone Close to You Experienced Abortion

Note: Not all of the questions will apply to your situation. It all depends on when you found out about the pregnancy and the abortion.

Before

When did you find out about the pregnancy?

What was your reaction?

What was her/their reaction?

Who else knew?

What role did you play, if any, in the decision to abort?

During

When and where did the abortion take place?

Did you accompany her/them to the clinic or doctor's office?

What was that like?

After

What happened right after the abortion?

Were you able to talk about it?

If so, with whom?

What happened in the days and weeks that followed?

What happened in the months and years that followed?

What did you feel immediately afterward?

What do you feel now?

How has the abortion impacted your life?

changed

tell your story

Build Support 12

Build Support

As you work through your own abortion experience or the abortion of someone close to you, it will be helpful to reach out to others for support.

The importance of telling your story to another person and receiving his or her support as you explore your emotions and identify your losses cannot be overestimated.

You don't need to make this journey alone.

In fact, I think it's best that you don't.

If you haven't shared your experience with anyone before or if past attempts to talk about it haven't gone well, then you may feel reluctant to reach out to someone.

This is certainly understandable. Sharing your experience entails some risk.

Perhaps your abortion is a secret.
Building a support system will require you to reveal your secret to at least one other person.

> *I dreaded sharing my secret.*
> *I thought that I would be judged harshly—*
> *that I would be looked at differently.*
> *Fortunately, my fears were unfounded.*

Perhaps you want to keep the abortion of a family member or friend private. This is an important consideration. Finding individuals who don't know the family member or friend may be preferable in this situation.

Because abortion is rarely discussed on a deeply personal level, you'll need to carefully consider who is safe to include in your support system.

> *If you haven't experienced abortion, you may want to consider how you can be a safe and supportive person for those who have.*

It may take some time to find the right person(s),
and it may be uncomfortable or painful at first.
But it's well worth the effort.

Some possibilities to consider for your support system:

- Family Members
- Friends
- Spiritual Counselor (such as a minister, priest, or rabbi)
- Support Group
- After Abortion Healing Resource
- Professional Therapist

In the space provided,
you can write the names of the people you're considering to be a part of your support system.

This is an initial list that can be revised later.

After you've listed the names of potential support system members,
there are some questions on the next few pages that you can ask yourself.
They'll help you reflect on each individual and his or her ability to support you.

This space is yours—feel free to write the names of whomever comes to mind.

NAMES

QUESTIONS TO CONSIDER

After reviewing these questions, you may want to remove some people from the list, and you may want to add others.

CONFIDENTIALITY

Will this person protect my confidentiality and the confidentiality of others who were involved in the abortion?

Has this person ever shared confidential information that I've told him or her in the past?

If this person has shared other confidential information, it may be best to seek out a person who's shown that he or she can be trusted with personal information.

Keep in mind that each abortion touches many people.

You may feel comfortable having the abortion become public knowledge, but the other participants may not. It's important to consider the privacy of all those impacted—the woman who had the abortion, her partner, their current spouses, their children, family members, and friends. It's important to protect their confidentiality as well.

LISTENING

Is this person a good listener?

Does this person automatically offer his or her opinion or advice?

A member of your support system should have the ability to listen well, ask questions if clarification is needed, and care for your overall well-being. Consider whether you've had difficulty with this person being a good listener in the past.

A person who is inclined to "fix" you or to minimize your experience won't be helpful.

AVAILABILITY

Does this person live close by?

Does this person always seem busy or have a busy schedule?

Will this person be available if a need arises at an odd time of the day or night?

In addition to being available to speak with you over the phone or through e-mail, a member of your support system should be available to meet with you in person from time to time. Consider the driving or walking distance to this person's home or business. Also consider if the person is available to respond within 24 hours to a phone or e-mail message.

Healing is unpredictable—you may not need support for days, weeks, or months at a time before going through an intense period of need that requires one or more members of your support system to connect with you frequently or at odd times.

HONESTY

Will this person be honest with you if he or she doesn't have the resources to be the support you need?

Will this person support you in finding other resources, such as support groups or professional resources, if he or she thinks this is in your best interest?

Sometimes a member of your support system may be aware that he or she is not equipped to adequately support you. This person needs to have honest and open communication skills and be willing to admit his or her limitations.

It's unlikely that one person will be able to meet all of your needs. As you move through the healing process, your support system will most likely grow.

INVOLVEMENT

Was this person involved in the abortion experience?

Keep in mind that some family members or friends may also be experiencing troubling emotions about the abortion. Until you've both dealt with the emotions and losses related to the abortion, it's best to seek someone else to be a part of your support system.

BELIEFS

Does this person have strong political beliefs about abortion?

Is this person an activist on either side of the issue?

A person's political beliefs or activism neither qualifies nor disqualifies him or her from being a part of your support system. However, it's important to consider whether a person will be able to look beyond his or her beliefs to respect your feelings and support you throughout your healing journey.

A person—whether he or she is a family member, friend, spiritual counselor, or professional therapist—who attempts to deny or minimize your experience will be unable to assist you as you seek to make sense of the abortion experience.

A person who urges you to publicly share your story before considering whether or not this is a healthy or appropriate step for you or for the others who've been impacted by the abortion will also be unable to assist you.

STARTING

As a concrete step, you may want to contact at least one person from your list today, just to set up a time to get together for an initial conversation about the type of supportive relationship you seek.

Starting is often the hardest part. Anxiety and even feelings of fear are natural.

This step will take some courage, but you can do it.

I've included some information about possible reactions you may encounter to help prepare you to move through this essential healing pathway.

Building your support system is important—
and important tasks often take some time and effort.

But before long, you'll find a person
or two
who will walk this journey with you.

You are not alone!

POSSIBLE REACTIONS FROM FAMILY MEMBERS OR FRIENDS

Keep in mind that when you reveal a past abortion,
a person's initial reaction may not be what you'd hoped.

If the abortion was a secret,

then the person may be shocked, hurt, or upset.

If the person knew about the abortion,
then he or she may be surprised to learn it's still affecting you.

Don't take someone's reaction—or lack of reaction—personally.

Because abortion is rarely talked about,
it's normal for people to be confused about what to do or say.

Mindy ("I Thought Life Would Be the Way It Was Before") was confused about how to react to friends who were having miscarriages and friends who were having abortions.

Priscilla's friends ("I Never Had the Chance to Know My Brother or Sister") "freaked out" when she tried to tell them about her parents' abortion. However, Priscilla's boyfriend was able to be supportive.

In most cases the person will overcome his or her initial awkwardness and support you throughout your journey.

You can help the members of your support system overcome their discomfort by sharing with them some specific ways that they can help you.

If this subject is new to them, then you may want to give them a copy of this book or refer them to the Abortion Changes You Web site (www.AbortionChangesYou.com).

Specific ways they can help you may include one or more of the following—

- *Listening to your story*
- *Calling you periodically just to see how you're doing*
- *Watching your children so you can have some time alone to work on the activities in this book*
- *Helping you locate a professional therapist or support group*
- *Driving you to an appointment or meeting*
- *Attending a support group with you*
- *If you believe in prayer—praying for you.*

In those cases where a person isn't able to offer you the support you need, don't give up!

You may want to approach another family member or friend on your list, or you may choose to seek support and counsel from a spiritual counselor, an after abortion healing resource, or a professional therapist instead.

> *The first person I chose to reach out to was a friend in Hawaii who didn't know my family. I made sure we were in a private place before telling her about the abortion. It took me a long time to get the words out because of my anxiety and my tears. But before I could ask her for anything, she was by my side and offering me support. I was so relieved!*

Explore Emotions 13

Explore Emotions

Exploring your feelings is an important part of working
through your abortion experience.

Denying, repressing, or pushing down your emotions may work
for a while;
but at some point,
you'll need to process your emotions in a safe environment.

Refusal to face your emotions surrounding a loss,
such as abortion,
can lead to unhealthy behaviors. (You'll read more about this in
the chapter called "Recognize Unhealthy Behaviors.")

People will experience a variety of emotions
at different times and
at different levels of intensity.

This may be due to a number of factors including age, gender,
cultural influences, and level of participation in the abortion.

You may already be in touch with your emotions,
or you may be numb to your emotions,

or you may be overwhelmed by your emotions.
Emotions may increase at particular times,
such as around the time of significant dates
or with certain reminders of the experience.

> *Around the anniversary of the expected due date of her grandchild, Ann ("My Wife Gets Depressed") has a rough time emotionally, while Brad ("I Often Wonder") experiences sadness when he sees little children.*

You may also find that you have different feelings regarding the same event
or that some feelings reoccur over time.

> *Juanita ("I Thought Life Would Be the Way It Was Before") experienced conflicted emotions of relief and sadness. Amber ("I Never Had the Chance to Know My Brother or Sister") was indifferent about her mother's first abortion, but angry and grief-stricken about her mother's second abortion.*

Wherever you're at, this space is for you to either start
or continue to explore the emotions associated with an
abortion experience.

Exploring your emotions takes work—it's often painful and draining.

Although you may wish to do some of the work on your own,
you'll benefit from communicating with your support system throughout the process.

If you find yourself becoming overwhelmed by your emotions, please visit AbortionChangesYou.com and use the Find Help locator to access support resources. Or use your phone book to locate professional therapists, after abortion healing resources, or church counseling programs in your area.

> *Two years after my abortion, the troubling emotions I experienced began increasing in frequency and intensity. I was so overwhelmed that I began contemplating suicide. Alarmed by what I was thinking about doing, I eventually went to see a professional therapist.*

IDENTIFY FEELINGS

This exercise can help you begin to explore your feelings by first putting a name to them.

Read through the list of possible emotions
and choose the ones that best describe how you feel.

You may choose emotions that you've felt at different times before, during, and after the abortion experience.

Or you may simply want to choose emotions that you're feeling right now or have felt in the past several days or weeks.

Feel free to circle or highlight the different emotions.

You may also want to jot down if you're feeling them right now,
if you've felt them in the past,
or if they tend to reoccur at certain times of the year.

If you're having trouble naming your emotions,
you may wish to try one of the activities suggested after the list of emotions.

If you've written your story, you may want to refer back to it, as it will most likely contain emotions that you felt before, during, and after the abortion.

If you're still unable to get in touch with your emotions, it may help you to talk to members of your support system and request their feedback.

Don't get discouraged.

If you've gotten into the habit of pushing down your emotions,
it will take awhile for you to start feeling them again.

If you're masking your emotions through the use of alcohol, illegal drugs, prescription drugs, an eating disorder, excessive work, and so on, then you'll need to address these behaviors (see "Recognize Unhealthy Behaviors") before you'll be able to successfully identify your emotions.

People process their emotions differently.
Activities that work for one person may not work for another.

Women may find that they're more inclined
to write or talk about their feelings,
while men may find it easier to express their emotions
through physical activities.

However, each person and each situation is unique.

Be patient,
give yourself time,
and remember that you are not alone.

Afraid
Alive
Alone
Angry
Anxious
Ashamed
Betrayed
Bleeding
Brave
Broken
Calm
Capable
Changed
Cleansed
Comforted
Confused
Dead
Degraded
Depressed
Determined
Dirty
Discouraged
Empowered
Empty
Encouraged
Exhausted
Fake
Forgiven
Forgotten
Fragile
Free
Frozen
Frustrated
Grateful
Grieving
Guilty
Happy
Haunted
Healing
Healthy
Heartbroken
Helpless
Hopeful
Hopeless
Hypocritical
Impatient
Invisible
Irrational
Isolated
Jealous
Joyful
Longing
Lost
Loved

Maternal
Miserable
Mourning
Naked
Needy
Neglected
Numb
Nurtured
Obsessed
Optimistic
Overwhelmed
Peaceful
Punished
Questioning
Rage
Raped
Raw
Ready
Rebellious
Reckless
Regretful
Relieved
Renewed
Resentful
Ruined
Sad
Safe
Selfish
Shocked
Sick
Spiritual
Struggling
Stuck
Supported
Sympathetic
Thoughtful
Threatened
Tortured
Ugly
Understood
Unloved
Unprepared
Unworthy
Uplifted
Used
Validated
Valued
Violated
Violent
Vulnerable
Weak
Welcomed
Worthless
Wounded

OTHER EMOTIONS

ACTIVITIES

If you're having trouble naming your emotions, then you may wish to try one of the activities suggested below.

Art
Draw, paint, make a collage, sculpt, take photographs, and explore your feelings through art

Fishing, Camping, Gardening
Connect with nature, explore the outdoors, and use the time for reflection

Meditation, Prayer, Retreat
For those with a background of faith, meditate or pray either privately or within a faith community

Poetry, Music
Write a poem or compose a song to explore your experiences and feelings

Walking, Running, Hiking
Outdoor physical activity can free your mind from other concerns for a time, allowing you to connect with any thoughts and feelings that may be deeply buried

You may want to keep these activities private,
or you may choose to share them with members of your support system.

JOURNAL

Now that you've identified some emotions,
you're invited to explore them through a journal entry or entries.

Connecting with your feelings is an important part of healing.

Describing your emotions may help you process the abortion and the impact it's had on you and on others in your life.

> *I think this is so important because most people feel a tangle of emotions surrounding an abortion.*
> *But identifying and describing the emotions helps untangle them and places order around what may feel chaotic.*

The length of the entry or entries is completely up to you—
you may write a few words,
a few paragraphs,
or a few pages.

You may want to explore one emotion at a time, or you may wish to describe groups of emotions.
Words can also be combined with sketches or pictures.

At the end of this book, you'll find additional space for journaling.
You can also use a notebook or your computer.

Your journal should be a private space just for you.

A place of complete honesty and transparency.

A place where you can record anything.

Saving your journal entries is suggested, as they may provide helpful information and insight throughout the healing process.

The space below is yours to begin exploring the feelings related to your abortion experience in freedom and privacy.

You can find additional space in the Journal section on page 250.

explore emotions

Identify Losses 14

Identify Losses

In the process of telling your story and exploring your emotions, you may have already identified losses that resulted from the abortion.

These losses may include one or more of the following—

- Loss of child, grandchild, brother or sister, niece or nephew
- Lost opportunity to parent or grandparent
- Lost or weakened relationship with parents, family members, or friends
- Spiritual loss—feeling far away from or angry toward God
- Loss of self-esteem or having a low opinion of yourself
- Loss of relationship with your partner
- Loss of dreams, goals, or vision for your life

The loss(es) you've experienced
or are experiencing
as a result of the abortion
are real.

Identifying and acknowledging these losses is an important step toward healing.

Minimizing or denying them will not only impede the healing process,
but it may also lead to unhealthy behaviors (see the next chapter).

Although this is a difficult step, you may feel a certain amount of relief when you're able to put a name to the loss(es) you've experienced.

It's also a comfort to know you're not alone.

Brad ("I Often Wonder") lost his marriage and his child; Susan ("We Made the Decision Together") lost joy and contentment in her and her husband's accomplishments; Carol ("My Wife Gets Depressed") came close to losing her daughter, Julie, to depression; Alex ("We Made the Decision Together") lost her child, her sister or brother, her niece or nephew, her fiancé, her dreams for the future, and her self-confidence.

Please use this space to identify your losses. To aid you in this process, you may wish to refer back to your story or any activities you completed while exploring your emotions (see the previous chapter).

LOSSES

ACCEPTING LOSS

Identifying and acknowledging your loss(es) is important. Deciding to accept and resolve them is even more important.

In fact, it's a decision to grieve them.

And the decision to grieve your losses
is a decision to feel pain.

Our culture tends to minimize grief by either
denying it
or promoting quick and efficient ways to deal with it.

However, neither of these strategies works
because grief is real
and grieving is a process.

Masking the reality of grief and pain
doesn't benefit those who are suffering from loss.

Your losses are real.
Your grief is real.
Your pain is real.

Your ability to move through the grieving process and to experience healing is also real.

Grieving rarely moves through a series of steps in a linear fashion.

Grief tends to intensify and diminish in cycles over a period of time.

People work through their grieving processes differently—some more quickly than others.

The intensity of feeling also varies from person to person.

The support of family and friends through this process of dealing with grief and loss is very helpful. However, family and friends aren't always willing or able to lend support to someone who's experiencing grief after an abortion.

My family was willing to lend support once they found out; but their own feelings of loss and grief as a result of the abortion undermined their ability to help me.

I believe I was also ineffectual in my attempts to comfort them because I was the cause of their loss. But over time, we found ways to comfort and support each other.

There are also times when people get stuck somewhere in the grief cycle,
and they find themselves unable to complete the process.

This is when the aid of a trained counselor or support group is recommended.

Please see the end of this chapter for more information about complicated grief.

As you move through the grieving process,
it will be helpful for you
to gather support from others,
to be patient with yourself,
to give yourself time and space to work through the process,

to understand that each person's journey is unique,
and to know the pain will diminish over time.

Journaling will be beneficial.

You may wish to write a symbolic letter that expresses your anger, sadness, disappointment, or betrayal to those who were involved in your abortion loss(es).

You may also wish to write a letter seeking their forgiveness.

WRITE A LETTER

You may feel anger,
sadness,
guilt,
or any number of emotions
toward your identified losses.

If you felt pressured into the abortion,
then you may harbor resentment toward those who were involved
or toward God for failing to rescue you.

Janet ("I Thought I Was Helping Her") used to blame her dad for pressuring her to have two abortions.

If you suggested the abortion
or felt as though you didn't do enough to encourage a different pregnancy outcome,
then you may feel guilt.

Zack ("I Thought I Was Helping My Girlfriend") carries tremendous guilt about the loss of his child, the loss of his relationship with his girlfriend, his drug use after the abortion, and his girlfriend's continued drug abuse.

Mary ("My Wife Gets Depressed") feels guilty that she didn't talk to her son, Ryan, about his request to have his girlfriend live with them. Mary feels it's her fault that her son went through so much pain and that his child wasn't born.

If a pregnancy was hidden from you until after the abortion,
you may feel anger or helplessness.

Mitch ("I Often Wonder") was angry that his girlfriend didn't tell him about the pregnancy until after she'd already had the abortion.

Your emotions may be directed outward
at other people or at God,
your emotions may be directed inward
at yourself,
or they might be directed toward
the child whose life was lost.

I found that anger toward my boyfriend and the others involved diminished quickly. What I couldn't shake was the anger I felt toward myself—anger that expressed itself in depression, an eating disorder, and eventually in the desire to commit suicide. My reaction was more extreme than others', but it does illustrate that anger turned inward isn't healthy and that it needs to be addressed.

You may desire forgiveness or you may want to blame or strike out at someone.

This is all a normal part of moving through the grieving process.

Writing a letter that expresses your feelings to the individuals involved,

It helps to get it out of your head and down on paper.

reading the letter to yourself,

Although reading the letter out loud can be very painful, it often starts the process of letting go of the negative emotions.

and then destroying the letter can be helpful.

You may need to write more than one letter.

Rather than writing one letter to encompass all of the losses and the individuals involved or impacted, I recommend writing a separate letter for each one.

You may even choose to write a letter to the child who was lost in the abortion.

I wrote more than one letter—including a letter to my aborted child. This may sound strange, but it was important for me to acknowledge the reality of my child's very brief life, as well as the lost opportunity for that child to be born and to grow up and to be enjoyed by my family.

These letters are not meant for sending or saving.

These letters are meant for your eyes only.

However, if a spiritual counselor, trained after abortion healing counselor, or professional therapist is part of your support system, then you may choose to read the letter(s) to this person or have him or her read the letter(s) to you. You may also wish to destroy the letter(s) in this person's presence.

DESTROY THE LETTER

In order to heal, you'll need to let go of the harmful emotions you feel toward yourself or toward others.

So now that you've written and read your letter, I encourage you to destroy it.
The act of destroying the letter symbolizes your willingness to let go of the anger,
shame,
or other harmful emotions.

The act of destroying the letter also symbolizes your willingness
to forgive and to accept forgiveness.

As the letter
is torn into little pieces,
imagine the harmful emotions toward others, yourself, or God

disintegrating.

The act of destroying the letter isn't nearly as important
as the decision you're making
to let go of the negative
and invite the positive into your life.

While the emotions may return,
your decision to move on will remain,
allowing you to continue moving forward toward healing.

SPIRITUAL ASSISTANCE

If you're dealing with anger, disappointment, guilt,
or shame in relation to God,
or if you're seeking forgiveness from God,
then you could benefit from receiving some spiritual counsel
or connecting with a faith community.

Taking such steps could also be beneficial if you're having trouble forgiving yourself or others.

You may feel hesitant about speaking to a minister, priest, or rabbi because you fear condemnation or judgment.

On the other hand, if your faith tradition defends or encourages abortion, then you may also be hesitant because you believe your pain might be minimized.

If you're unsure about the reaction you'll receive from members of your faith community,
then you may wish to seek out an after abortion healing resource that is religiously affiliated.

Many people who have experienced abortion find great comfort and hope through the prayers and support of others and in the assurance of God's love and forgiveness.

Note: The Abortion Changes You Web site provides a listing of after abortion healing resources that are religiously affiliated, as well as some churches that provide similar services.

After abortion healing resources often provide individual guidance, as well as group support or retreat style workshops that specifically address the grief and loss that's experienced as a result of abortion.

Please visit the Web site AbortionChangesYou.com and use the Find Help locator to access information about these resources, or use your phone book to find similar resources in your area.

COMPLICATED GRIEF

There are times when people get stuck somewhere in the grief cycle and they find themselves unable to complete the process.

While it's important not to impose an expected time frame for healing, you also don't want to allow yourself to remain stuck for too long because then it's that much harder to move through the grieving process.

If you've experienced any of the following symptoms for more than one month, then you may be developing impacted grief, or complicated grief, or some other psychological complication.

This typically feels like you're "stuck" in your grief and unable to move forward in your life.

To rule out these possibilities, consultation with a trained counselor is recommended.

POSSIBLE SIGNS OF COMPLICATED GRIEF

- Anxiety
- Difficulty concentrating
- Difficulty sleeping
- Dulled sense of feeling
- Fear or avoidance of children
- Fixating on another child
- Flashbacks
- Inability to recall parts of the event
- Nightmares
- Rage

Recognize Unhealthy Behaviors 15

Recognize Unhealthy Behaviors

Abortion can produce strong emotions
—so strong that it's natural to wish to avoid them or to mask them.

Denying,
repressing,
or pushing down
these emotions may work for a while,
but continued refusal to face the emotions surrounding a loss such as abortion can lead to more difficulties and more pain.

Abortion represents significant loss(es) in a person's life.

Identifying and acknowledging these losses is an important step toward healing.

On the other hand, minimizing or denying them and the grief they produce will not only impede the healing process, but it may also lead to unhealthy behaviors.

Because our culture tends to minimize or deny the loss and grief associated with abortion, it's easy to understand why so many of us avoid the unpleasant emotions regarding our own abortions or the abortion of someone close to us.

Unhealthy behaviors that may have been present before the abortion are likely to be continued or accelerated after the abortion.

Zack ("I Thought I Was Helping Her") and his girlfriend were drug users before the abortion. Afterward their drug use spun out of control. Zack was able to stop, but unfortunately his girlfriend became addicted.

In the beginning, unhealthy behaviors may be used as protective measures either to cope with or mask painful emotions or to deny grief and loss. If the behaviors are repeatedly used, then they may begin to take on a compulsive life of their own with seemingly no connection to the abortion.

After her fiancé left, Alex ("We Made the Decision Together") started working more and socializing to avoid being alone in her apartment. What started out as a strategy to avoid loneliness and feel better about herself, eventually took on a life of its own and led to substantial debt and loss of self-esteem.

Unhealthy behaviors may be a daily occurrence, or they may occur periodically.

Sometimes unhealthy behaviors are triggered by certain events,
such as the anniversary of the abortion
or the expected due date of the child.

Whether or not you think these behaviors are related to an abortion experience, extra assistance such as a 12-Step program or group, spiritual assistance, or professional counseling is needed to regain your well-being.

Examples of unhealthy behaviors are listed on the following pages, along with some helpful resource information.

In addition to the resources listed under each behavior, you may also wish to contact after abortion healing resources, which will often provide individual guidance, as well as group support or retreat style workshops.

Please visit the Web site AbortionChangesYou.com and use the Find Help locator to access information about after abortion healing resources, or use your phone book to find similar resources in your area.

Even if you don't think you're participating in unhealthy behaviors,
please take a moment to look over the list.

If you suspect you may be using some of these behaviors, please take the time to visit a Web site or make a phone call to determine if you need assistance.

If it turns out that you're participating in any of the behaviors,
you may need to focus your attention on recovery before continuing the healing process.

Remember, you are not alone!

RESOURCES FOR DEALING WITH UNHEALTHY BEHAVIORS

Resources are offered for referral purposes only. Inclusion does not constitute endorsement of a resource. If a resource is omitted, it is not meant to indicate disapproval of that resource. The quality of care of services provided by any resource listed is in no way guaranteed. The author has not investigated the resources, or confirmed the accuracy of any information provided regarding resources. All information comes from the resources themselves, and may change without notice.

ANGER

National Child Abuse Hotline
1-800-4-A-CHILD (1-800-422-4453)
www.childhelp.org/get_help
Available 24 hours a day and 365 days a year, a hotline for children or for adults who are concerned about children who may be suffering abuse or neglect. Completely confidential, but be aware that if you call from a mobile (cell) phone, the call may show up on your bill. The counselors won't know who you are unless you tell them.

National Domestic Violence Hotline
1-800-799-SAFE (1-800-799-7233)
1-800-787-3224 (TDD)
www.ndvh.org
Also available in Spanish, this hotline offers help 24 hours a day and 365 days a year to those in crisis situations. The Web site offers information about safety planning, referrals, crisis intervention, action items, teen dating abuse, and more.

ANXIETY

Depression Awareness, Recognition, Treatment Helpline
1-800-421-4211

National Alliance on Mental Illness
www.nami.org
Alliance to help those suffering from mental illness, as well as their loved ones. Includes information on a variety of mental illnesses including bipolar disorder, depression, schizophrenia, dissociative disorders, personality disorders, eating disorders, panic disorder, seasonal affective disorder, Tourette's syndrome, and post-traumatic stress. Also offers support for loved ones, information on legislation, and resources in different states.

Panic Disorder Information Hotline
1-800-64-PANIC (1-800-647-2642)

COMPULSIVE DISORDERS

Mayo Clinic: Obsessive-Compulsive Disorder (OCD)
www.mayoclinic.com/health/obsessive-compulsive-disorder/DS00189
Web site explains OCD, helps identify signs, and leads a person to find treatment.

CUTTING/SELF-ABUSE

Self-Injury Hotline
S.A.F.E. (Self-Abuse Finally Ends) Alternatives Program
1-800-DON'T-CUT (1-800-366-8288)
www.selfinjury.com
S.A.F.E. is a nationally recognized treatment approach, professional network, and educational resource base, which is committed to help people achieve an end to self-injurious behavior. Self-injury is known by many names, including self-abuse, self-mutilation, deliberate self-harm, and parasuicidal behavior.

DEPRESSION

Depression Awareness, Recognition, Treatment Helpline
1-800-421-4211

International Foundation for Research and Education on Depression (iFred)
www.ifred.org
Offers research and support for those suffering from depression and fighting against the stigma associated with depression.

Mayo Clinic: Depression
www.mayoclinic.com/health/depression/DS00175
Web site addresses the causes, risk factors, signs and symptoms, and treatment of depression, as well as coping skills.

National Alliance on Mental Illness
www.nami.org
Alliance to help those suffering from mental illness, as well as their loved ones. Includes information on a variety of mental illnesses including bipolar disorder, depression, schizophrenia, dissociative disorders, personality disorders, eating disorders, panic disorder, seasonal affective disorder, Tourette's syndrome, and post-traumatic stress. Also offers support for loved ones and resources in different states.

National Depression and Manic Depression Association
1-800-82-NDMDA (1-800-826-3632)
www.ndmda.org
Offers help—information, research, and recovery—for individuals and loved ones of those living with mood disorders.

DIFFICULTY GETTING CLOSE TO OR CARING FOR YOUR CHILD/CHILDREN, PARTNER, FAMILY MEMBERS/FRIENDS

American Counseling Association
www.counseling.org
Helps you find a licensed counselor in your area. You can search by topic.

National Directory of Marriage and Family Counseling
www.counsel-search.com
This Web site offers FAQs and articles about counseling, how to choose a counselor, how to get your money's worth, and a locator tool to help you find a marriage counselor in your area.

EATING DISORDERS

American Anorexia/Bulimia Association, Inc. (AABA)
212-575-6200
Offers referrals to treatment and information.

National Association of Anorexia Nervosa and Associated Disorders (ANAD)
847-831-3438 (The hotline is open between 9 a.m. and 5 p.m. CST, Monday through Friday.)
www.anad.org
Offers referrals to treatment and information.

National Call Center for At-Risk Youth
1-800-USA-KIDS
Available 24 hours for teens.

National Eating Disorders Association (NEDA)
1-800-931-2237 (toll-free information and referral helpline)
www.nationaleatingdisorders.org
For answers, information, and nationwide referrals.
Available 8:30 a.m.–4:30 p.m. PST, Monday through Friday.

National Eating Disorder Referral and Information Center
858-481-1515
www.edreferral.com
Provides information and treatment resources for all forms of eating disorders. Their goal is to provide assistance, in the form of information and resources, to those suffering from eating disorders in order to help them start on the road to recovery and healthy living.

Overeater's Anonymous
505-891-2664
www.overeatersanonymous.org
Offers referrals to local chapters and information.

FROZEN EMOTIONS

American Counseling Association
www.counseling.org
Helps you find a licensed counselor in your area. You can search by topic.

National Directory of Marriage and Family Counseling
www.counsel-search.com
Web site offers FAQs and articles about counseling, how to choose a counselor, how to get your money's worth, and a locator tool to help you find a marriage counselor in your area.

GAMBLING AND OVERSPENDING

Compulsive Gambling Center
924 East Baltimore St.
Baltimore, MD 21202
1-800-LOST-BET (1-800-567-8238)
www.lostbet.com

Debtors Anonymous
General Service Office
P.O. Box 920888
Needham, MA 02492-0009
781-453-2743
Fax: 781-453-2745
www.debtorsanonymous.org
Debtors Anonymous is a fellowship of men and women who share their experience, strength, and hope with each other. Their primary purpose is to stop debting one day at a time and to help other compulsive debtors to stop incurring unsecured debt.

National Council on Problem Gambling (NCPG)
1-800-522-4700 (24-hour, national confidential helpline)
216 G Street NE, Suite 200
Washington, DC 20002
202-547-9204
Fax: 202-547-9206
ncpg@ncpgambling.org
www.ncpgambling.org
The mission of the National Council on Problem Gambling is to increase public awareness of pathological gambling, ensure the widespread availability of treatment for problem gamblers and their families, and to encourage research and programs for prevention and education.

MOOD SWINGS

Depression Awareness, Recognition, Treatment Helpline
1-800-421-4211

National Alliance on Mental Illness
www.nami.org
Alliance to help those suffering from mental illness, as well as their loved ones. Includes information on a variety of mental illnesses including bipolar disorder, depression, schizophrenia, dissociative disorders, personality disorders, eating disorders, panic disorder, seasonal affective disorder, Tourette's syndrome, and post-traumatic stress. Also offers support for loved ones and resources in different states.

National Depression and Manic Depression Association
1-800-82-NDMDA (1-800-826-3632)
www.ndmda.org
Offers help—information, research, and recovery—for individuals and loved ones of those living with mood disorders.

Panic Disorder Information Hotline
1-800-64-PANIC

OVERWORKING

Workaholics World Service Organization
P.O. Box 289, Menlo Park, CA 94026-0289
510-273-9253
wso@workaholics-anonymous.org
www.workaholics-anonymous.org
A 12-Step program for individuals who hope to stop working compulsively, it offers a 20-question test you can take to see if you might be a workaholic.

PHOBIA

Mayo Clinic
www.mayoclinic.com/health/phobias/DS00272
Provides help in understanding the causes, signs and symptoms, treatment options, and better coping methods for people who suffer from phobias.

Medline Plus
www.nlm.nih.gov/medlineplus//phobias.html
Also in Spanish, this Web site offers help with identifying and managing phobias.

RISKY BEHAVIORS (RISK-TAKING)

American Association of Suicidology
202-237-2280
www.suicidology.org
The American Association of Suicidology is an education and resource organization.
They don't provide direct services. However, if you are in crisis and need immediate help, please call 1-800-273-TALK (8255), The National Suicide Prevention Lifeline provides access to trained telephone counselors, 24 hours a day, 7 days a week.

American Foundation for Suicide Prevention (AFSP)
1-888-333-AFSP (1-888-333-2377)
www.afsp.org
AFSP is the only national not-for-profit organization exclusively dedicated to understanding and preventing suicide through research and education, and to reaching out to people with mood disorders and those affected by suicide.

National Suicide Prevention Lifeline
1-800-273-TALK (1-800-273-8255)
www.suicidepreventionlifeline.org
The National Suicide Prevention Lifeline is a 24-hour toll-free service available to all those in suicidal crisis who are seeking help. Individuals seeking help will be routed to the closest possible provider of mental health and suicide prevention services.

Self-Injury Hotline
S.A.F.E. (Self-Abuse Finally Ends) Alternatives Program
1-800-DON'T-CUT (1-800-366-8288)
www.selfinjury.com
S.A.F.E. is a nationally recognized treatment approach, professional network, and educational resource base, which is committed to help people achieve an end to self-injurious behavior. Self-injury is known by many names, including self-abuse, self-mutilation, deliberate self-harm, and parasuicidal behavior.

Yellow Ribbon Suicide Prevention Program
1-800-SUICIDE (1-800-784-2433)
1-800-999-9999

SELF-MEDICATING WITH ALCOHOL

Al-Anon/Alateen Family Group Headquarters, Inc.
1-800-344-2666 (U.S.)
1-800-443-4525 (Canada)
Provides information about Al-Anon/Alateen and referrals for local meetings. Available 8 a.m.–6 p.m. EST, Monday through Friday.

Alcohol Treatment Referral Hotline
1-800-ALCOHOL (1-800-252-6465)
Provides 24-hour help and referrals for people with concerns about alcohol or drug use.

Alcoholics Anonymous World Services, Inc.
212-870-3400
Provides information about AA and worldwide referrals to local meetings. Available 8:30 a.m.–4:45 p.m. EST, Monday through Friday.

Center for Substance Abuse Treatment National Drug and Alcohol Treatment Referral Service (24 hours)
1-800-662-HELP (1-800-662-4357)
Can link the caller to a variety of hotlines that provide treatment referrals.

National Council on Alcoholism and Drug Dependence (NCADD) Hopeline
1-800-622-2255
Will refer the caller to a local affiliate office of the National Council on Alcoholism and Drug Dependence. Callers can also leave their names and addresses to receive written information about alcohol and other drug abuse. Touch-tone phone is required. Available 24 hours.

SELF-MEDICATING WITH DRUGS

Center for Substance Abuse Treatment National Drug and Alcohol Treatment Referral Service (24 hours)
1-800-662-HELP (1-800-662-4357)
Can link the caller to a variety of hotlines that provide treatment referrals.

Marijuana Anonymous (MA) World Services
1-800-766-6779
Provides information about MA and referrals to local meetings. Available 24 hours (voice mail).

Nar-Anon World Services
1-800-477-6291
Provides information about Nar-Anon and worldwide referrals to local meetings. Available 9 a.m.–4 p.m. PST, Monday through Thursday.

Narcotics Anonymous (NA)
818-773-9999
Provides information about NA and worldwide referrals to local meetings. Available 8 a.m.–5 p.m. PST, Monday through Friday.

National Council on Alcoholism and Drug Dependence NCADD Hopeline

1-800-622-2255

Will refer the caller to a local affiliate office of the National Council on Alcoholism and Drug Dependence. Callers can also leave their names and addresses to receive written information about alcohol and other drug abuse. Touch-tone phone is required. Available 24 hours.

National Drug Abuse Hotline

1-800-662-HELP (1-800-662-4357)

SEXUAL DYSFUNCTION OR SEXUAL ACTING OUT

Sexaholics Anonymous International Central Office

P.O. Box 3565
Brentwood, TN 37024
615-370-6062
866-424-8777
Fax: 615-370-0882
saico@sa.org
www.sa.org

Sexual Addicts Anonymous (SAA)
1-800-477-8191 from the U.S. and Canada
+1-713-869-4902 elsewhere
ISO of SAA
P.O. Box 70949
Houston, TX 77270
USA
info@saa-recovery.org
www.saa-recovery.org
Provides information and questions about the SAA program, help when you can't find a meeting, or other problems. The phone is answered between 10 a.m. and 6 p.m. CST, Monday through Friday. Voice mail is available at all other times.

ISO of SAA
P.O. Box 70949
Houston, TX 77270
USA
info@saa-recovery.org
www.saa-recovery.org

National Call Center for Addiction Intervention Resources
1-800-561-8158
www.addictionintervention.com
Includes resources for gambling, eating disorders, sex

addiction, co-occurring addictions, alcohol and drug abuse, adolescent issues, mental health issues, and so on.

SUICIDAL THOUGHTS

The National Suicide Prevention Lifeline
1-800-273-TALK (8255)

Yellow Ribbon Suicide Prevention Program
1-800-SUICIDE (1-800-784-2433)

American Association of Suicidology
202-237-2280
www.suicidology.org
The American Association of Suicidology is an education and resource organization.
They don't provide direct services. However, if you are in crisis and need immediate help, please call 1-800-273-TALK (8255), The National Suicide Prevention Lifeline provides access to trained telephone counselors, 24 hours a day, 7 days a week.

American Foundation for Suicide Prevention
1-888-333-AFSP (1-888-333-2377)
www.afsp.org

AFSP is the only national not-for-profit organization exclusively dedicated to understanding and preventing suicide through research and education, and to reaching out to people with mood disorders and those affected by suicide.

National Suicide Prevention Lifeline
1-800-273-TALK (1-800-273-8255)
www.suicidepreventionlifeline.org
The National Suicide Prevention Lifeline is a 24-hour toll-free service available to all those in suicidal crisis who are seeking help. Individuals seeking help will be routed to the closest possible provider of mental health and suicide prevention services.

Teen Helpline
1-800-400-0900

TeenLine
1-800-522-8336

UNHEALTHY OR ABUSIVE RELATIONSHIPS

Break the Cycle and The Safe Space
5200 W. Century Blvd. #300
Los Angeles, CA 90045
310-286-3366

1-888-988-TEEN (8336) Available from 1–4 p.m. PST, Mondays and Fridays
www.breakthecycle.org
www.thesafespace.org
Two Web sites from one organization linked together to help empower youth. The Safe Space includes help with identifying a troubled relationship, how to help a friend, developing a safety plan for your relationship, and information about your legal rights, contacting the police, and getting a restraining order. It also includes ways to volunteer and what parents should know about teen dating abuse. Break the Cycle engages, educates, and empowers youth to build lives and communities free from domestic and dating violence.

National Child Abuse Hotline
1-800-4-A-CHILD (1-800-422-4453)
www.childhelp.org/get_help
Available 24 hours a day and 365 days a year, it's a hotline for children or for adults who are concerned about children who may be suffering abuse or neglect. Completely confidential, but be aware that if you call from a mobile (cell) phone, the call may show up on your bill. The counselors won't know who you are unless you tell them.

National Domestic Violence Hotline
1-800-799-SAFE (1-800-799-7233)
1-800-787-3224 (TDD)
www.ndvh.org
Also available in Spanish, this hotline offers help 24 hours a day and 365 days a year to those in crisis situations. The Web site offers information about safety planning, referrals, crisis intervention, action items, teen dating abuse, and more.

National Runaway Switchboard
1-800-RUNAWAY (1-800-786-2929)
www.1800runaway.org
Provides free transportation for those wishing to return home, as well as shelter for those for whom going home is not an option.

VIOLENCE

Break the Cycle and The Safe Space
5200 W. Century Blvd. #300
Los Angeles, CA 90045
310-286-3366
1-888-988-TEEN (8336) Available from 1–4 p.m. PST, Mondays and Fridays
www.breakthecycle.org/
www.thesafespace.org/

Two Web sites from one organization linked together to help empower youth. The Safe Space includes help with identifying a troubled relationship, how to help a friend, developing a safety plan for your relationship, and information about your legal rights, contacting the police, and getting a restraining order. It also includes ways to volunteer and what parents should know about teen dating abuse. Break the Cycle engages, educates, and empowers youth to build lives and communities free from domestic and dating violence.

Coalition to End Family Violence
805-656-1111
1-800-300-2181 Bilingual
Help with domestic violence, anger management issues, sexual abuse, and so on.

National Child Abuse Hotline
1-800-4-A-CHILD (1-800-422-4453)
www.childhelp.org/get_help
Available 24 hours a day and 365 days a year, it's a hotline for children or for adults who are concerned about children who may be suffering abuse or neglect. Completely confidential, but be aware that if you call from a mobile (cell) phone, the call may show up on your bill. The counselors won't know who you are unless you tell them.

National Domestic Violence Hotline
1-800-799-SAFE (1-800-799-7233)
1-800-787-3224 (TDD)
www.ndvh.org
Also available in Spanish, this hotline offers help 24 hours a day and 365 days a year to those in crisis situations. The Web site offers information about safety planning, referrals, crisis intervention, action items, teen dating abuse, and more.

National Runaway Switchboard
1-800-RUNAWAY (1-800-786-2929)
www.1800runaway.org
Provides free transportation for those wishing to return home, as well as shelter for those for whom going home is not an option.

recognize unhealthy behaviors

Begin Healing 16

Begin Healing

If you've told your story,
built a support system,
explored your emotions,
identified and begun grieving your losses,
and recognized any unhealthy behaviors,
then you've made significant progress!

You've made the decision to be honest
about your experience
and the impact it's had on your life
and the lives of those around you.

You've made a decision to grieve,
to feel pain,
to discard unhealthy behaviors—
you've made the decision to begin healing.

You've also made the decision to let go of the loss(es)—to survive your loss.

Dealing with your loss will ultimately lead to positive personal growth.

If you haven't done so already, it's time to make another decision—
to let go of the pain.

Surprisingly, this isn't as easy as it sounds.

Sometimes we get used to the pain,
sometimes we hang on to the pain so we don't forget the loss,
and sometimes we're afraid to move on.

> *I find that I'm willing to hang on to something that is painful yet familiar, rather than letting go to embrace the unknown—even if I think the unknown will be better.*

Letting go of the pain means very different things to different people.

Letting go may mean letting go of broken relationships that can't be mended.

Letting go may mean letting go of some of the dreams for your life.

Letting go may mean letting go of the child who perished.

Your loss is no less real once you decide to let go of the pain.

On the contrary,
the loss takes its place as a part of your unique history—
no longer hidden or suppressed,
but integrated into your past and contributing to who you are now
and who you will continue to be in the future.

This can often mean being a person who has a special understanding of and compassion for others who've experienced the kind of loss(es) you have.

> *Throughout the healing process, you've already been turning your own pain into hope for others who are experiencing their own loss and grief. In time, you'll be an incredible resource for those needing support and encouragement.*

You may want to write in your journal about your decision to let go of the pain,
or you may want to memorialize your decision in some other way.

You may also wish to date and initial the statement below.

"I've decided to let go of my pain.
I've decided to continue the process of healing."

This doesn't signify that healing is concluded,
it simply signifies your willingness to complete the journey.

Journaling will continue to be an important tool, and your support system will continue to aid you greatly. You may also need to work on any unhealthy behaviors.

Healing doesn't mean you have it all together.
It means you're taking purposeful steps to go through a process.

Loss can sometimes take on different meanings over time.

William and Ann ("My Wife Gets Depressed") initially grieved over the loss of their grandchild and the impact the abortion had on their daughter. However, they were comforted by the thought of enjoying future grandchildren.

But decades later, when Lisa didn't have more children, they began to grieve the fact that they'd never have grandchildren.

In the future you may experience other emotions regarding the abortion; however, when that happens, you'll have many resources to draw upon to help you deal with those emotions.

Dealing with the loss and grief of the abortion will also prepare you to deal with other losses that inevitably occur in life. I've certainly found this to be true.

You'll also have the skills to process them and integrate them into your life.

You won't need to fear them,
avoid them,
or repress them;
you'll be able to embrace them and keep moving forward.

REACHING OUT

Reaching out brings hope to others and renewed health and healing to yourself.

There are countless ways you can help others, including sharing your story of healing,
telling a friend or family member who's experienced abortion about this book,
or volunteering in your community.

Volunteer opportunities include—

- Helping an elderly or disabled neighbor
- Running errands for a friend or family member who is ill or overwhelmed
- Serving in a soup kitchen
- Libraries
- Museums
- Places of worship
- Mentorship programs

If you wish to share your story [2], then you may submit Word, PDF, or JPG files to the Web facilitator [3] at AbortionChangesYou.com. You may also wish to share a poem, song lyrics, or a photo of an artistic creation or activity that depicts your healing process.

[2] If you submit a story, then it will be helpful if you share some background about the abortion, the impact of the abortion, how you dealt with the experience, and any healing resources that were helpful for you or for your family. Please do your best to protect the privacy of those involved by removing any information that could reveal their identities.

[3] If your submission is posted, identifying details will be removed to protect anonymity.

If you'd like to share your story or activity, but prefer that it not be posted on the Web site for others to see, then please e-mail your file to me directly at MichaeleneFredenburg@AbortionChangesYou.com.

I know it's sometimes helpful to share with another person, and I'd be honored to see your creation.

Thank you for including me in your journey.

I hope you've found
or are in the process of finding
peace.

I also hope you'll join me in reaching out to others
who are trying to make sense of their abortion experiences
and offering them the simple message that they aren't alone
and there is hope.

There is always hope.

Michaelene

Michaelene

AFTERWORD

Changed: A Therapist's Reflection

Changed: A Therapist's Reflection

DEAR FELLOW READER OF *CHANGED*:

As I begin my reflections regarding this book, I want to identify myself as someone who has also been impacted by abortion. All of us who have encountered the reality of abortion in our lives have been changed. As a man, I am obviously unable to experience the incredibly significant and personal impact of this medical procedure directly. But I have been impacted by abortion indirectly—and also very personally.

I am a professor of psychology who has been teaching college courses in human sexuality for many years. In my position, it can be easy to develop a somewhat detached view of many of the issues that are usually addressed in such courses. This mindset is often identified as the "ivory tower perspective," a typically somewhat disengaged, supposedly more objective, but often rather unfeeling view of and response to issues that can be of vital significance and very personal to those involved. However, my experience with abortion has definitely taken me out of any "ivory tower" position I might have held in the past.

In addition to teaching for nearly 40 years, I have been a practicing licensed psychotherapist who has worked with individuals, couples, and families. Within the context of my therapy work, I have been touched by the abortions that have taken place in the lives of my clients. Furthermore, I have been touched by the situations of my university students who have dealt with unplanned pregnancies. And finally, I have been touched within my relationships with individuals and couples who are very near and dear to me as they have experienced or contemplated an abortion. So while my own experiences have been more indirect, they have nevertheless been very real and significant to me personally.

As such, I definitely agree with Michaelene's statement that abortion changes us. We have come to experientially understand that even though abortion involves a decision on someone's part, that decision is only one of many important points along the journey. We must also consider what happens to us after the decision is implemented—primarily, the fact that we have been changed; secondarily, how we have been changed; and thirdly, where we are presently—within ourselves—regarding that change.

Reflecting on how we have been changed by abortion seems to be a function of how close we were to the abortion itself. So let us consider the degree of closeness that each of us has experienced.

You are obviously the closest if you are a woman who has experienced an abortion. My heart goes out to you as you live with that reality. You understand because you have gone through what Michaelene has described so meaningfully in this book. My sincere hope is that you have already begun the restorative process she has outlined and that you have experienced some healing and growth. If not, then I want to encourage you to give yourself permission to do so as soon as you are ready.

Human nature is not conducive to thriving in the midst of pain and suffering, although life in an imperfect world forces us to experience such encounters throughout our lives. Nevertheless, we can find ourselves tolerating our uncomfortable feelings because we are afraid our conditions might worsen if we give our full attention to their source. However, my years of clinical experience have led me to conclude that the opposite is true: The sooner we begin addressing such issues, the sooner we are able to experience healing and the increased freedom to live in the present for the sake of the future, rather than living in such a way that merely attempts to avoid the pain of the past.

Regardless of where you are in that process, as a woman who has had an abortion, you have experienced the greatest impact and have carried that reality within your soul via the memories, thoughts, and feelings that span what led up to, what happened during, and what followed the event. You must have felt so lonely as you carried this load without someone by your side. You are the only one who can know how hard it has been. And I hope you no longer feel totally alone, now that you have made an initial connection by reading this book. I also hope you will find a sense of support and comfort as you engage with the other readers of *Changed* who are pursuing their healing journeys by engaging in the pathways suggested by Michaelene.

Perhaps you are among another group of people—those who did have others walk beside them throughout the experience. Hopefully, those helping individuals were supportive and understanding. But for at least some of you, one or more of these people only added to the difficulty of your experience. Oftentimes, people who are aware of our situation believe they are helping us. But not being in the same place we are, they can only respond from wherever they are. Thus, we often sense a lack of true understanding and genuine support. Whatever your circumstances have been, my hope is that you'll find a more encouraging experience as you continue your journey.

The group of people that is the next closest to the abortion event are the men involved in the pregnancy. From the men who participated in the decision to abort to those who learned of the event only after the fact, each one has unique and personal memories, thoughts, and feelings. With whom can a man share these private responses to his history? Personal sharing is typically more challenging for men because oftentimes we do not have safe and trustworthy relationships with other men with whom we can bare our souls. So if you are a man who has not shared your experience with someone else, I believe the various pathways described by Michaelene can significantly assist you as you begin to work through your experience. And, again, I hope you will not feel alone during the process but will sense a sort of kinship with the rest of us—a part of that total community of "the changed."

Beyond the two individuals who are the most intimately involved in the abortion, there are the rest of us. We find ourselves somewhere in the array of the changed who are identified in this book: friends, siblings, grandparents, and other family members. While our individual experiences are varied, I believe we can identify with one another with at least some degree of experiential understanding that can help us feel compassion and provide support for one another.

I share Michaelene's understanding of how the growth and healing process is unique to each of us. Elements such as the point of readiness to actively enter into the process, the pace of the journey, the variations within the journey, specific steps that need to be taken, and the time it takes to complete the journey differ for everyone. But there are some common themes that help us identify with one another, as I have already noted.

So how can we know where we are in the process? When we plan to travel somewhere by car, we can use a mapping Web site on the Internet to spell out every turn we'll need to make, the distance between each of those turns, the total length of the trip, and the approximate time it will take us to complete the journey. But emotional journeys are far less precise. They rarely go the shortest possible distance or take the minimum possible time. Nor is the pace consistent, sometimes moving quite rapidly with significant insights and the processing of feelings, and other times seeming to move quite slowly or hardly moving at all.

During those slow times, in particular, we might begin to feel discouraged and even wonder if we should have attempted the journey, or wonder if it will ever be completed. My years of experience tell me that it is important to do our best to remain committed and, as we are able, take the next step. With such commitment and a willingness to pursue the journey step by step, I believe the outcome is inevitable—we will grow, we will experience healing, and we will arrive at a point where we can once again actively pursue the opportunities that life presents—living in the present for the sake of the future.

Some might ask, "But what about those very intense feelings that I experience? Are they real? Are they normal? And what can I do about them?" I can assure you that every feeling within you is real and has a source. In fact, this is true about all of our feelings in response to all of life's experiences. This is the very normal nature of feelings. Some feelings that we experience in the present, however, are old feelings, feelings left over from past experiences. As such, these feelings are valid for the "then and there," but much less so—or not at all—for the "here and now."

Some feelings may feel strange and abnormal, but often these can be a "normal response to an abnormal situation or experience." And that is what makes our feelings about the abortion so powerful—the abortion was an "abnormal" experience, while all the feelings that follow it are normal.

We best deal with the array of our feelings by giving them voice, whether that involves sharing them with a trusted friend or other helping person (such as a spiritual leader or a counseling professional) or writing them out in some form of journaling activity, as Michaelene suggests. But we cannot resolve our feelings without facing them honestly—as we are ready and willing to do so. Here again, we can identify with and offer support and encouragement to one another, even if only within our own hearts, as we pursue our own healing. I hope you will let yourself sense, as well as feel within yourself, the support and encouragement that we collectively offer to one another through our common experience of reading *Changed* and pursuing the growth and healing pathway.

When we find ourselves experiencing feelings that are beyond our ability to voice and understand, particularly if those feelings are frightening to us, we will likely need to seek professional assistance to make sense of those feelings and to find ways to move through them and ultimately move beyond them to a state of acceptance and hope. As distressing as these episodes can be, each one is an opportunity to grow and experience further healing. Again, since there are no pre-drawn and trustworthy road maps showing the journey to completion, we need to courageously follow the pathway that opens itself before us, one step at a time. This is literally a "road map in the making" that will be complete only at the end of the journey. Or, at the very least, it is only as complete as the steps we have taken so far.

I stated earlier that we each have our own unique experience, but it may be helpful to also consider that women and men tend to experience and process their feelings somewhat differently. As a general rule, women tend to be more aware of their feelings, and they often find it easier to articulate their feelings with another person. In contrast, men tend to experience and process their feelings more privately, sometimes having difficulty admitting those feelings to themselves, let alone to other men.

Sadly, men (still generally speaking) often do not establish safe and trustworthy relationships with other men. So they either need to make the development of such a relationship part of their journey, or they may turn to a woman they know as a trustworthy friend. But such opposite-sex sharing can also have its pitfalls. I recommend that we men do whatever we need to do in order to find another trustworthy man with whom we can share and process our feelings. This is a lesson I thankfully learned long ago, and I have found this practice to be tremendously helpful to me in my own processing and growth over the years. One way to begin is by consulting a counseling professional or seeking the guidance of a spiritual leader.

My final thoughts are these: There is always hope to be found as we take the courageous first step to remember what we have experienced and felt as a result of a particular experience or a collection of experiences. And as we are willing to remember, we can begin working through our remembered experience(s) and taking additional steps by giving some form of voice to those memories, to our subsequent thoughts, and to the inevitable feelings that are generated. Processing these collected memories, thoughts, and feelings, particularly with the assistance of others, can not only provide deeper self-understanding and insight into what we have been through, but the combination of these efforts (which typically need to include self-forgiveness and forgiveness of others as we are ready to do so) can also free us from the burdens of the past, converting those "millstones around our necks" to "stepping stones" that help elevate us to new levels of insight, understanding, and compassion, while preparing us to live more richly in the future.

Just as our bodies are designed to experience a healing process following an injury or illness, the same is true of our souls. It is not a matter of "if" we can find healing, but "when" we will begin the healing journey. My hope for each of you is that you will not only pursue that journey as soon as you are ready, but that you will find the increasing freedom and restoration of hope and joy that are available to us by means of our respective healing journeys.

Let me express a final word to those of you who do not identify yourself as one of the people I have written to above, as well as to those who have read this book in order to prepare themselves to help someone with his or her journey after an abortion experience. Thank you for being there for that person and for seeking information that will help you to be as effective a supporter as you can be. I have found that when we are at a point in which we can come alongside and assist others, we not only become a source of blessing to that person, but we are also richly blessed ourselves—and particularly so if we are passing on what we have already experienced in our own journeys. Paraphrasing a first-century writer, we are able to bring comfort and help to others—and of the very nature that we ourselves have experienced—because we encountered such comfort and help on our own pathways.

May we all be sources of comfort and support as we reach out to one another in the midst of the challenges of life. And may you be richly blessed.

Gary H. Strauss, EdD
Professor of Psychology, Rosemead School of Psychology, Biola University

Journal

Journal

MY STORY **DATE**

changed

journal

PERSONAL IMPACT	DATE

journal

IMPACT ON OTHERS DATE

journal

FEELINGS DATE

journal

LOSS(ES)	DATE

journal

GRIEVING	DATE

journal

UNHEALTHY BEHAVIORS DATE

journal

HEALING PROCESS **DATE**

journal

REACHING OUT DATE

journal

HOPE **DATE**

journal

RANDOM REFLECTIONS DATE